SPANISH II
UNIT EIGHT

CONTENTS

I.	EL AUTOMÓVIL	2
	Listening Exercises I	16
II.	GRAMMAR REVIEW	21
	Listening Exercises II	35
III.	THE PRESENT PERFECT TENSE	37
	Listening Exercises III	51
IV.	THE PLUPERFECT TENSE	53
	Listening Exercises IV	64
V.	REVIEW OF UNIT SEVEN	71
VI.	GEOGRAPHY OF CENTRAL AMERICA AND THE CARIBBEAN	81
	VOCABULARY LIST	89

Author: Katherine Engle, M.A.
Managing Editor: Alan Christopherson, M.S.
Revision Editor: Christine E. Wilson, B.A., M.A.
Illustrators: Steve Ring, Dawn Tessier, Annette Walker, Kyle Bennett, Joann Cumming

Graphic Designers: Annette Walker
Alpha Omega Graphics

804 N. 2nd Ave. E., Rock Rapids, IA 51246-1759
© MMI by Alpha Omega Publications, Inc. All rights reserved.
LIFEPAC is a registered trademark of Alpha Omega Publications, Inc.

All trademarks and/or service marks referenced in this material are the property of their respective owners. Alpha Omega Publications, Inc. makes no claim of ownership to any trademarks and/or service marks other than their own and their affiliates', and makes no claim of affiliation to any companies whose trademarks may be listed in this material, other than their own.

SPANISH II - UNIT EIGHT
INTRODUCTION

By studying the automobile, you will continue learning, in Spanish, about methods of transportation. Section One presents basic automotive parts (the gas tank and the bumper, for example), their functions, and how to care for each part. You will even be able to express, in basic terms, how to finance a car. Because cars are an important part of our lifestyle, it is only natural to include a study of them in this series.

A presentation of ordinal numbers will help you to enumerate and prioritize information in Spanish.

A study of the past participle will teach another way to use verb forms in sentences. Past participles can be used in Spanish as adjectives or as verb phrases. You can use the verb *sentarse* to express *He is seated* as well as *He sits down*. The dual usage of the past participle expands your ability to express yourself without requiring further acquisition of vocabulary terms.

Once the past participle as an adjective is reviewed, you will put it to work in two more verb tenses: the present perfect and the pluperfect. These are past tenses and give the foreign language student more options of expressing past events.

Numerous activities will provide comprehensive practice in writing, listening, and reading.

OBJECTIVES

Read these objectives. These objectives tell what you should be able to do when you have completed this Unit.

1. Use vocabulary pertaining to the automobile.
2. Identify basic auto parts and describe their functions in Spanish.
3. Use ordinal numbers.
4. Be more proficient in the formation and dual usage of the past participle.
5. Use the present perfect and the pluperfect verb tenses. These are compound tenses, so they use the past participle as part of their verb form.
6. Be more proficient in using the future and conditional tenses and vocabulary related to air travel.
7. Be familiar with the geography of Central America and the Caribbean.

I. EL AUTOMÓVIL

In the last unit, you reviewed vocabulary pertaining to air travel. In Unit Eight, you will take a look at our most popular way to travel: the car.

el automóvil	el coche
el auto	el carro

LAS PARTES DE UN AUTOMÓVIL

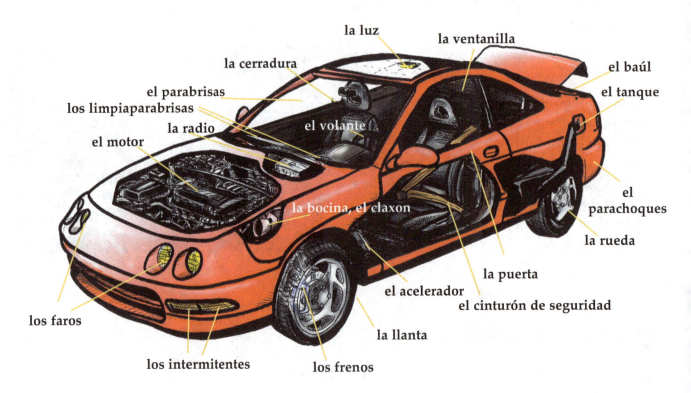

   Make the following.

1.1 Purchase a package of 3" x 5" cards and create a set of flashcards for yourself to review for each of the four sections of this vocabulary unit. Start each day's vocabulary lesson with a quick review of the flashcards. Quiz a partner, if you wish, or just yourself. Split your cards into the easy and the difficult words as you go through each of the vocabulary words.

✔ Adult check _____
                    Initial   Date

Where would you locate these auto parts? Choose the correct answer.

1.2
1. ¿Dónde está el parabrisas?
   a. en la parte delantera del coche
   b. dentro del coche
   c. en el baúl

2. ¿Dónde están los intermitentes?
   a. en el parabrisas
   b. en el motor
   c. cerca de los faros

3. ¿Dónde está el volante?
   a. muy cerca del motor
   b. debajo del tanque
   c. dentro del coche

4. ¿Dónde se encuentra el parachoques?
   a. debajo del coche
   b. sobre el coche
   c. al fondo del coche

5. ¿Dónde está el baúl?
   a. dentro del coche
   b. al fondo del auto
   c. cerca del volante

6. ¿Dónde están los frenos?
   a. muy cerca de las ruedas
   b. dentro de las llantas
   c. encima del motor

7. ¿Dónde está la radio, típicamente?
   a. a la izquierda del volante
   b. a la derecha del volante
   c. sobre el parabrisas

8. ¿Dónde están las llantas?
   a. alrededor de las ruedas
   b. en el motor
   c. entre los faros

9. ¿Dónde está la bocina?
   a. en la ventanilla
   b. debajo del motor
   c. en medio del volante

10. ¿Dónde está el acelerador?
    a. debajo del volante
    b. a la derecha del parachoques
    c. junto a la radio

 Identify the following car parts in Spanish.

1.3 a. _____

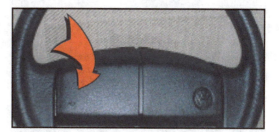

b. _____

c. _____

d. _____

e. _____

f. _____

g. _____

h. _____

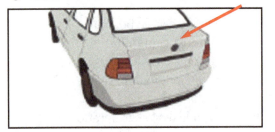

i. _____

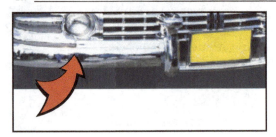

j. _____

k. _____

l. _____

m. _____

n. _____

o. _____

Complete the translations by filling in the correct term from the new vocabulary.

1.4 a. The car's window is broken. _____ del _____ está rota.

b. The horn doesn't work. _____ no funciona.

c. Is there another tire in the trunk? ¿Hay otra _____ en _____?

d. Don't forget to turn on the headlights. No te olvides de encender _____.

e. The gas station attendant puts gas in the tank and washes the windshield. El empleado de la gasolinera echa gasolina en _____ y lava _____.

f. He honked the horn when the brakes failed. Tocó _____ cuando fallaron _____.

g. Turn on the turn signal. Enciende _____.

h. I need new wipers. The old ones don't clean the windshield well. Necesito _____ nuevos. Los viejos no limpian bien _____.

i. His car is so old the bumper fell off. Su coche es tan viejo que _____ se cayó.

j. The dome light doesn't work, but the radio does. _____ no funciona, pero la radio sí.

 Quiz yourself! Label as many parts of this car as you can from memory. Once you have practiced all the terms, use your notes to complete the assignment.

1.5

Adult check _____
                    Initial   Date

Algunas actividades y funciones de un coche y sus partes

Review the following terms:

El motor puede...

funcionar (bien/mal) – *to function, work*
arrancar – *to start*

El volante es para...

guiar – *to steer*
doblar – *to turn*
virar – *to turn, swerve*
dirigir – *to steer, direct*
conducir, manejar – *to drive*

Los frenos son para...

parar – *to stop*
reducir la velocidad – *to reduce speed, slow down*

Los faros, los intermitentes
y la luz son para...

señalar – *to signal*
iluminar – *to illuminate, light (up)*
mostar – *to show*

acelerar – *to accelerate*

El acelerador es para…

limpiar – *to clean*

Los limpiaparabrisas son para…

proteger – *to protect*
impedir las heridas – *to prevent injuries*

El cinturón de seguridad es para…

llevar – *to carry*
abrir – *to open*
cerrar – *to close*

El baúl es para…

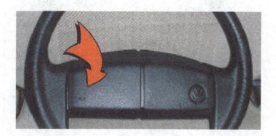

tocar – *to sound (honk)*
avisar – *to warn*

La bocina es para…

Algunas actividades para cuidar de un coche

lavar – *to wash*   **mantener** – *to maintain*

llenar el tanque – *to fill the tank*   **reparar** – *to repair*

cambiar el aceite – *to change the oil*   **arreglar** – *to fix*

 Decide if the following statements about the functions of certain auto parts are true or false. Mark the true statements *V* (for *Verdadero*) and the false ones *F* (for *Falso*). Correct the false statements in Spanish.

1.6 a. _____ El parabrisas para el coche.
_____

b. _____ Los faros iluminan la oscuridad por la noche.
_____

c. _____ El volante sirve para guiar el coche.
_____

d. _____ Se llevan las maletas en la rueda.
_____

e. _____ El acelerador quita el agua del parabrisas.
_____

f. _____ Es importante llenar el tanque mucho.
_____

g. _____ Se usa el acelerador para reducir la velocidad del coche.
_____

h. _____ La radio protege a los pasajeros durante un accidente.
_____

i. _____ Cambiar el aceite es buena manera de mantener el coche en buenas condiciones.
_____

j. _____ Se debe tocar la puerta solamente cuando sea necesario.
_____

 Identify each pictured car part and its function in a complete Spanish sentence.

1.7

a. _____   b. _____
_____   _____

c. _____ d. _____

_____   _____

e. _____ f. _____

_____   _____

g. _____ h. _____

_____   _____

i. _____

_____

✓ Adult check _____
              Initial   Date

Give each Spanish term defined below.

1.8 a. la ventana del auto _____
    b. echar gasolina en el coche _____
    c. ir más lentamente _____
    d. lo que se abrocha _____
    e. el vehículo _____
    f. por donde se entra en el interior del coche _____
    g. las luces grandes y blancas de un coche _____
    h. la parte donde se llevan las maletas _____
    i. "el corazón" de un coche _____
    j. resolver los problemas de un coche _____
    k. iluminar _____
    l. poner fin al movimiento del coche _____
    m. manejar _____
    n. virar _____
    o. dar información de algo malo que puede pasar _____

Translate the sentences from one language to the other.

1.9 a. El intermitente señala que el coche vira a la derecha.
    _____

    b. Llene el tanque, por favor.
    _____

    c. Nuestros cinturones de seguridad nos protegeron bien en el accidente.
    _____

    d. Abre la puerta y cierra el baúl.
    _____

    e. El coche no funciona porque el motor no arrancó esta mañana.
    _____

    f. Slow down!
    _____

    g. She can change the tires.
    _____

h. I'll steer the car to the left.

i. I keep my car in good condition by changing the oil often.

j. He signaled left, but he turned right.

Necesitas un auto?

Entonces, necesitas…

adquirir – *to acquire*

obtener – *to get, obtain*

alquilar, arrendar (e-ie) – *to rent*

pedir prestado – *to borrow*

un préstamo – *a loan*

pagar a plazos – *to make (monthly) payments*

la mensualidad – *monthly payment*

¿Ya tienes coche?

Recuerda…

obedecer las leyes – *to obey the laws*

tener cuidado – *to be careful*

prestar atención – *to pay attention*

(no) chocarse con – *(not) to crash into*

dar un paseo – *to go for a ride*

Fill in the missing Spanish term.

1.10   a.   Recientemente, hice un viaje de negocios. Tuve que _____ un coche porque yo fui a otra ciudad en avión.

b.   Felipe visitó el banco. Él necesitaba _____ porque no tenía quince mil dólares para comprar un vehículo nuevo.

c.   Es necesario _____ las leyes de tráfico o se le da una multa (a ticket).

d.   Para Ud. es imposible pagar todo el dinero de pronto. Puede _____ .

e.   El Sr. Chepo no obedeció el límite de velocidad. _____ un árbol.

f.   Un buen conductor siempre _____ mientras maneja.

g.   Los frenos no funcionan. Es peligroso porque yo no puedo _____ el coche.

h.   Abre _____ y pone las maletas por dentro.

i.   Hay demasiado viento. Cierra _____ .

j.   El joven está emocionado por _____ su primer coche.

Review the vocabulary for this lesson. Write the number of the picture on the next page beside each question it answers.

1.11

1.

2.

3.

4.

5.
6.
7.
8.
9.
10.

a. ¿En qué dibujo pide un préstamo? _____
b. ¿En qué dibujo se lava un coche? _____
c. ¿En qué dibujo se obedecen las leyes de tráfico? _____
d. ¿En qué dibujo se llena el tanque? _____
e. ¿En qué dibujo repara el coche? _____
f. ¿En qué dibujo se da un paseo? _____
g. ¿En qué dibujo se señala a la derecha? _____
h. ¿En qué dibujo se adquiere un carro nuevo? _____
i. ¿En qué dibujo se choca? _____
j. ¿En qué dibujo se acelera el coche? _____

Answer the questions in complete Spanish sentences.

1.12 a. ¿Dónde se echa la gasolina? _____

b. ¿Cómo se guía un coche? _____

c. ¿Cómo se mantiene el coche en buenas condiciones? (give **2** different answers) _____
_____

d. ¿Cómo se obtiene el dinero para comprarlo? _____

e. ¿Cómo se ilumina la calle? _____

f. ¿Cómo se evita un accidente? (give **2** different answers) _____
_____

g. ¿Cuál es más importante, el motor o los frenos? Explica. _____
_____

Use the following passage to practice your reading and writing skills in Spanish. Read the passage out loud. Answer the comprehension questions that follow.

1.13   Estoy listo para vender mi coche. Había una vez que funcionaba bien. No usaba mucha gasolina y se podía dirigirlo fácilmente. Solamente tenía que lavarlo y cambiar el aceite.

Hoy el coche es un desastre. Me parece que siempre estoy comprando gasolina. Los limpiaparabrisas no funcionan bien. Le falta mucha pintura. Los frenos hacen mucho ruido. Los parachoques están en malas condiciones. Cuando trato de acelerar el coche, no va muy rápidamente. Quiero venderlo pronto pero hay un problema más: ya sé que no recibiré muchos dólares por este coche, pero necesito uno para viajar al trabajo y ir por el pueblo.

1. How old must this car be? _____
   a. less than five years
   b. more than ten years
   c. It's brand new.

2. What is this car missing? _____
   a. the brakes
   b. gasoline
   c. a lot of paint

3. How must the author of this story feel presently? _____
   a. proud
   b. frustrated
   c. calm

4. What part of the car doesn't always work? _____
   a. the windshield wipers
   b. the brakes
   c. the gas pedal

5. How is the author going to get rid of this car? _____
   a. Leave it at work.
   b. Leave it in town.
   c. Sell it quickly.

▶ **Respond to each question in at least three complete Spanish sentences.**

1.14 a. Summarize the story told on the previous page. _____
_____
_____
_____
_____
_____

b. Should the author sell the car or spend money to repair it? Explain your answer. _____
_____
_____

c. Should the author be driving this car now? Why? _____
_____
_____

d. What would you pay for this car? Why? _____
_____
_____

LISTENING EXERCISES I

Exercise 1. Identify the picture you hear described by writing the number of the question next to it.
[CD–E, Track 1]

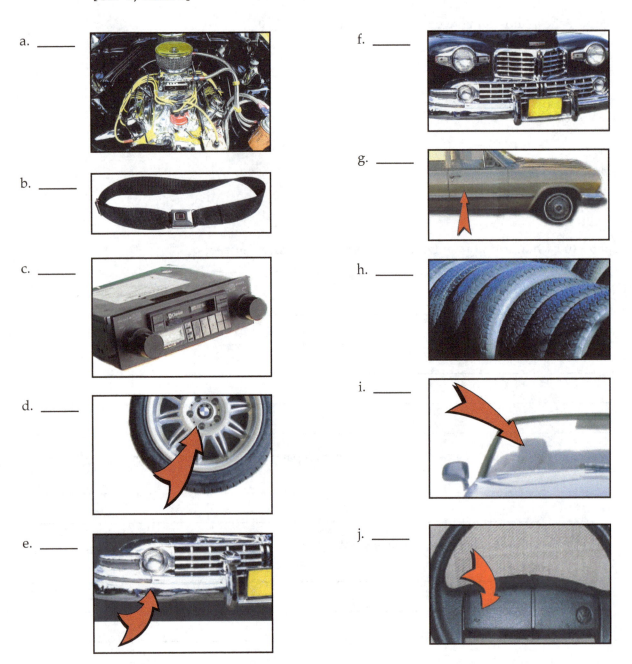

Exercise 2. Decide which term would most logically complete the sentences you hear. Circle the correct letter.
[CD–E, Track 2]

1. a. alquilas
   b. te chocas
   c. obedeces

2. a. pagar cada mes
   b. prestar atención
   c. limpiar

3. a. pide un préstamo
   b. reduce la velocidad
   c. se para

4. a. tiene cuidado
   b. acelera
   c. adquiere

5. a. Lleva
    b. Rompe
    c. Maneja

6. a. llena
    b. lleva
    c. llanta

7. a. repara
    b. arranca
    c. para

8. a. ilumina
    b. toca
    c. abre

9. a. dobla
    b. para
    c. escucha

10. a. quitar
    b. reducir la velocidad
    c. mostrar

Exercise 3. Identify which part of the car is best described by the definitions you will hear. Write the letter of the matching sentence next to the appropriate car part. [CD–E, Track 3]

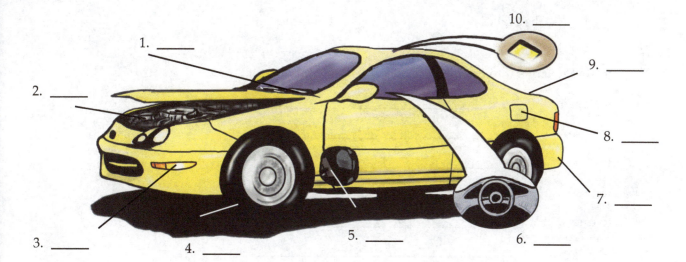

 Review the material in this section in preparation for the Self Test. The Self Test will check your mastery of this particular section. The items missed on this Self Test will indicate specific areas where restudy is needed for mastery.

SELF TEST 1

1.01 **Matching.** (1 pt. each)

1. _____ the tire   a. la bocina
2. _____ the horn   b. manejar
3. _____ to acquire   c. doblar
4. _____ the (dome) light d. llenar
5. _____ to turn   e. la llanta
6. _____ to rent   f. la luz
7. _____ to fill   g. los faros
8. _____ to drive   h. los frenos
9. _____ the headlights   i. alquilar
10. _____ the brakes   j. adquirir

1.02 **Translate the terms into Spanish.** (1 pt. each)

a. the engine   _____
b. to borrow   _____
c. the wheel   _____
d. to turn   _____
e. to direct   _____
f. to stop   _____
g. to pay attention   _____

1.03 **Translate the terms into English.** (1 pt. each)

a. el baúl   _____
b. el tanque   _____
c. obedecer   _____
d. chocarse con   _____
e. el parachoques   _____
f. el parabrisas   _____
g. señalar   _____
h. el aceite   _____

1.04 **Choose the correct function for each auto part.** (1 pt. each)

1. el baúl _____
   a. arrancar
   b. llevar
   c. virar

2. el motor _____
   a. iluminar
   b. alquilar
   c. funcionar

3. los intermitentes _____
   a. reparar
   b. señalar
   c. mantener

4. la cerradura _____
   a. avisar
   b. proteger
   c. adquirir

5. el volante _____
   a. acelerar
   b. reducir la velocidad
   c. dirigir

6. el acelerador _____
   a. aumentar la velocidad
   b. virar
   c. tocar

7. el limpiaparabrisas _____
   a. llenar
   b. abrir
   c. quitar

8. el cinturón de seguridad _____
   a. iluminar
   b. proteger
   c. avisar

9. el tanque _____
   a. llevar
   b. cerrar
   c. llenar

10. la bocina _____
    a. virar
    b. avisar
    c. parar

1.05 **Translate the following phrases into Spanish.** (2 pts. each)

a. I fill the tank. _____

b. In order to (*Para*) obey the law, he slows down. _____

c. You honk the horn. _____

d. He doesn't stop the car. _____

e. I needed a loan, because I bought a car. _____

f. The motor doesn't work. _____

g. The headlights light up the street. _____

h. She changes the car's oil. _____

i. Use the brakes! Stop! _____

j. They didn't pay attention. They crashed into a house. _____

1.06 **Write the Spanish terms defined.** (1 pt. each)

a. obtener dinero del banco _____

b. adquirir un coche por unos días _____

c. la parte del coche llena de aire _____

d. notar todos los detalles (*the details*) _____

e. hacer limpio _____

f. poner aceite nuevo _____

g. doblar _____

h. dar una señal _____

i. dar protección _____

j. una ventana del coche _____

52/65

Score _____
Adult check _____
            Initial   Date

II. GRAMMAR REVIEW

ORDINAL NUMBERS

As the name implies, ordinal numbers denote in what order things are (first, fifth, etc.). Read the summary of the race.

Hace unas tres horas que empezó el maratón. Ahora los atletas están a punto de terminar. Parece que #18 es el **primero**, seguido del #20, el **segundo**. #12 es la **tercera**.

#63 es la **cuarta** atleta que va a terminar este evento. Próximo viene #31, el **quinto**. #2 es la **sexta** y #8 es el **séptimo**. #10 es la **octava**. El **noveno** es #51, y por fin, #14 viene en el **décimo** lugar.

 List in order the highlighted ordinal numbers from the passage; then translate into English.

2.1 _____

_____

You have noticed that some of these terms end in -*o* and some in -*a*. Grammatically, this means that ordinal numbers agree in gender with their nouns, which are normally singular.

Examine two sentences from the passage:

#12 es la **tercera**. #63 es la **cuarta** atleta que va a terminar este evento.

First, translate them:

#12 is the third. #63 is the fourth athlete that is going to finish this event.

Ordinal numbers may stand alone in a sentence (*the third*), but when they are paired directly with a noun (*the fourth athlete*), they are placed directly in **front** of the noun.

Apart from their meanings, you have learned three facts about using ordinal numbers in a Spanish sentence: (1) ordinal numbers agree in gender with the noun to which they refer, (2) ordinal numbers may stand alone, and (3) ordinal numbers are placed directly in front of the nouns.

Practice what you have learned so far. Write the correct agreeing ordinal number in front of each noun.

2.2   a.   the fifth lap: la _____ vuelta

   b.   the ninth day: el _____ día

   c.   the second wave: la _____ ola

   d.   the first (man): el _____

   e.   the sixth time: la _____ vez

   f.   the tenth class: la _____ clase

   g.   the seventh car: el _____ coche

   h.   the third (lady): la _____

   i.   the eighth month: el _____ mes

   j.   the fourth school: la _____ escuela

 Use the calendar to answer the following questions in complete Spanish sentences. Note that Spanish calendars normally start on Monday, rather than Sunday.

2.3   a.   ¿Cuál es el quinto día?
   _____
   _____

   b.   ¿Cuál es el noveno día?
   _____
   _____

   c.   ¿Cuál es el segundo día?
   _____
   _____

   d.   ¿Cuál es el sexto día?
   _____

   e.   ¿Cuál es el cuarto día?
   _____

   f.   ¿Cuál es el octavo día?
   _____

noviembre

L	M	M	J	V	S	D
				1	2	3	4
5	6	7	8	9	10	11
12	13	14	15	16	17	18
19	20	21	22	23	24	25
26	27	28	29	30		

g. ¿Cuál es el séptimo día?
_____

h. ¿Cuál es el décimo día?
_____

▶ **Read the next two questions** *carefully* **before answering.**

2.4 a. ¿Cuál es el **tercer** día?
_____

b. ¿Cuál es el **primer** día?
_____

Do you notice something different regarding these? The difference is that they dropped the *-o*. The gender of the noun *día* is masculine.

The Spanish ordinal numbers "first" (*primero*) and "third" (*tercero*) are the only two that **drop the final "o"** before **masculine singular nouns**.

▶ **Fill in the blanks with the agreeing form of either** *primero* **or** *tercero*.

2.5 a. la _____ vez (first)   f. la _____ oportunidad (first)
     b. el _____ señor (third)   g. el _____ camino (third)
     c. la _____ parte (third)   h. el _____ amor (first)
     d. la _____ puerta (first)   i. la _____ fila (first)
     e. el _____ trabajo (first)   j. la _____ cita (third)

When working with ordinal numbers after *tenth* (e.g. thirteenth, twenty-fifth, etc.), use cardinal numbers. For example:

> **Ella vive en la calle treinta.** She lives on Thirtieth Street.
> **Tengo que leer el capítulo quince.** I have to read Chapter 15 (the fifteenth chapter).
> **Ella es la señora treinta y cinco.** She is *the 35th lady*.

Note that cardinal numbers are written **after** the noun when they take on the function of an ordinal number. Also, cardinal numbers, when used in this capacity, do not agree in number and gender with the noun they modify.

Finally, ordinal numbers, when paired with an agreeing definite article, can function as an adjective (that modifies a noun), or alone, as a pronoun (that replaces a noun).

> **La sexta silla es azul.** The sixth chair is blue.
> **La sexta es azul.** The sixth (one) is blue.

Sexta refers to *la silla*; thus its form is feminine singular, in order to agree with *silla*, when used as an adjective (in the first sample sentence) or alone, as a pronoun (in the second sample sentence).

 You and a friend are window shopping. The two of you are making choices about what you see in the window. Write a sentence that expresses your choice by using an ordinal number + definite article construction and the cues provided.

2.6   a.   ¿Qué mochila te gusta más? (the second one)

___

       b.   ¿Te gusta el tercer vestido o el quinto vestido? (the fifth one)

___

       c.   ¿Qué par de zapatos prefieres? (the eighth one)

___

       d.   ¿Qué estéreo comprarías? (the first one)

___

       e.   ¿Qué son los aretes más bonitos? (the second one and the ninth one)

___

       f.   ¿Te gusta el séptimo disco compacto o el cuarto disco compacto? (the fourth one)

___

       g.   ¿Qué camisa te gusta más? (the tenth one)

___

       h.   ¿Qué libro leerías? (the sixth one)

___

THE PAST PARTICIPLE

Examples of the past participle in English are verbs such as *broken, written, finished, seated*, etc. These are all actions that have occurred in the past.

Some examples of the past participles of English infinitives include:

to buy	bought
to read	read
to water	watered
to pay	paid
to travel	traveled
to direct	directed
to understand	understood
to write	written
to do	done
to say	said

 Use three of the above participles to write three English sentences.

2.7 a. _____

b. _____

c. _____

✔ Adult check _____
                              Initial   Date

Now, look at the Spanish equivalents of the first seven past participles given above.

comprar	comprado
leer	leído
regar	regado
pagar	pagado
viajar	viajado
dirigir	dirigido
comprender	comprendido

You have learned enough about verb conjugations to be able to tell how to form the past participle. **Note that the *-ar*, *-er*, or *-ir* was removed from the end of each infinitive.** The ending *-ado* was added to the AR infinitives and *-ido* was added to the ER and IR infinitives.

 Choose the correct translation of each participle.

2.8 1. caminado _____
   a. walking
   b. walks
   c. walked

2. encontrado _____
   a. found
   b. founded
   c. finding

3. permitido _____
   a. permit
   b. permitting
   c. permitted

4. salido _____
   a. left
   b. leaving
   c. would leave

5. comido _____
   a. ate
   b. eaten
   c. eating

6. archivado _____
   a. was filing
   b. filed
   c. files

7. sonado _____
   a. rung
   b. dreamed
   c. rang

8. cortado _____
   a. cutting
   b. would cut
   c. cut

9. jugado _____
   a. play
   b. played
   c. plays

10. comprado _____
    a. buys
    b. bought
    c. brought

 In the first blank, write the past participle of each infinitive. In the second blank, translate the participle.

2.9

	INFINITIVE	PAST PARTICIPLE	TRANSLATION
a.	cantar		
b.	vender		
c.	mirar		
d.	sentir		
e.	pedir		
f.	colgar		
g.	aprender		
h.	tener		
i.	preferir		
j.	dar		

In summary, a regular past participle verb form in English ends in -ed. In Spanish, however, the past participle ending depends on the verb form: regular AR verbs end in -ado, but regular ER and IR verbs end in -ido.

Let's now turn our attention to past participles with spelling changes or irregular forms. Verbs ending in -eer put an accent mark over the -i- in the past participle form. For example, creer ("to believe") becomes creído ("believed"). Verbs ending in -aer also put an accent mark over the -i- in the past participle form. For example, traer ("to bring") becomes traído ("brought"). This accent mark over the -i- forces the "i" to be stressed when spoken.

Write the past participles of these infinitives. Remember where to place the written accent. NOTE: *Oír* is also included in this group—*oído*.

2.10
a. caer (to fall) _____
b. poseer (to possess) _____
c. traer (to bring) _____
d. creer (to believe) _____
e. atraer (to attract) _____
f. leer (to read) _____

 Below is a list of infinitives that take an irregular past participle. They must be memorized. Write the English definition of the past participle after each word.

2.11

a. abrir	abierto	
b. cubrir	cubierto	
c. decir	dicho	
d. escribir	escrito	
e. hacer	hecho	
f. imprimir	impreso	
g. morir	muerto	
h. poner	puesto	
i. resolver	resuelto	
j. romper	roto	
k. ver	visto	
l. volver	vuelto	

It's important to remember that any compound verbs of these infinitives (verbs that actually contain these words in the roots) also follow the irregular pattern. For example: *componer* becomes *compuesto*.

27

Write the past participle of these irregular infinitives.

2.12

a. descubrir	
b. describir	
c. deshacer	
d. imponer	
e. devolver	

There are three other past participle forms to keep in mind.

dar (to give)	dado (given)
ir (to go)	ido (gone)
ser (to be)	sido (been)

Complete the translations by filling in the spaces with a past participle.

2.13
a. I've already read the rules. Ya he _____ las reglas.

b. He's seen that movie often. Ha _____ esa película muchas veces.

c. They have gone to the game. Han _____ al partido.

d. Oh no! You have broken the lamp! ¡Ay de mí! Has _____ la lámpara.

e. She would have set the table by now. Ya habría _____ la mesa.

f. The book was written by Manolo. El libro fue _____ por Manolo.

g. They've never returned their books on time. Nunca han _____ sus libros a tiempo.

h. She has fallen and broken her ankle. Se ha _____ y se ha _____ el tobillo.

i. The school was opened in 1902. La escuela fue _____ en 1902.

j. My mom had made dinner for us when we arrived. Mi madre había _____ la cena para nosotros cuando llegamos.

k. We have given a lot of money to that church. Hemos _____ mucho dinero a esa iglesia.

l. The coffee has been delicious, but today it's bitter. El café ha _____ muy rico, pero hoy es amargo.

Rewrite the given sentences using the past participle form of each given infinitive. Make any other necessary changes. Then, translate the new sentence into English.

2.14 1. El hombre está sentado en la manta. The man is seated on the blanket. (cubrir)

   a. _____
   b. _____

2. Jorge ha bajado del avión. Jorge has gotten off the plane. (subir)

   a. _____
   b. _____

3. Marina ha roto la cama. Marina has broken the bed. (hacer)

   a. _____
   b. _____

4. Se han leído sus palabras en todas partes del mundo. His words have been read all over the world. (creer)

   a. _____
   b. _____

5. Javier ha hecho una torta. Javier has made a cake. (comer)

   a. _____
   b. _____

6. Ellos han visitado el monumento. They have visited the monument. (ver)

   a. _____
   b. _____

7. Se han escrito los apuntes este año. The notes were written this year. (imprimir)

   a. _____
   b. _____

8. Esta canción es cantada en muchas naciones hoy. This song is sung in many nations today. (oír)

   a. _____
   b. _____

9. Ha muerto allí recientemente. He has died there recently. (vivir)

   a. _____
   b. _____

10. El regalo es devuelto el lunes. The gift is returned on Monday. (dar)

    a. _____
    b. _____

Up until this point, you may have noticed that these past participles have been translated without any subject; that is, *roto* translates only as "broken" and is not associated with *yo, tú,* etc. Even though a past participle is formed from an infinitive and communicates action, it cannot function in a sentence alone, like a verb form. **Participles must have helping verbs** within a sentence.

Some examples of helping verbs in English include *is, was, were, have, had, has, am, be, being, been,* and *are.*

In Spanish, when past participles are used with the verbs *ser* and *estar* (both meaning "to be"), they may function as adjectives. When they are used as an adjective, they must agree in number and gender with the noun they modify. Observe the following example.

La puerta está cerrada. The door is closed.

The past participle *cerrada* comes from *cerrar*. The part of the sentence that *cerrada* describes is *la puerta*. Why, then, is *cerrada* feminine? Because it is used as an adjective and describes a noun. This noun is feminine singular, so *cerrada* has to be made feminine singular.

Here's another example.

Nosotros estamos sentados a la derecha de Pedro. We are seated to the right of Pedro.

Sentados comes from the infinitive *sentar* and agrees with *nosotros*. Thus, its form is masculine plural in this case.

 Use the past participles of the given infinitives and the verb *estar* to write descriptive sentences about the pictures.

2.15 a. cerrar   b. morir

_____   _____

_____   _____

       c. parar   d. romper

_____   _____

_____   _____

e. herir

___

f. lavar

___

g. encender

___

h. facturar

___

i. escribir

___

j. mojar (to be wet)

___

Sometimes the construction *ser* + a past participle can be used in the place of the impersonal *se* to express the passive voice. This construction, however, is not nearly so commonly used as the one with *se*.

> **Se pone el libro sobre la mesa. / El libro es puesto sobre la mesa.**
>
> The book is put on the table.
>
> **Se venden muchas legumbres en este mercado. / Muchas legumbres son vendidas en este mercado.**
>
> Many vegetables are sold in this market.

 Create new passive voice expressions for each sentence. Use the verb *ser* and the past participle to change each sentence.

2.16   1.   El libro *fue escrito* por Meléndez.

        a. was bought   _____

        b. was burned   _____

        c. was published _____

2. Mamá *fue escuchada* por toda la familia.

   a. was called _____

   b. was helped _____

   c. was visited _____

3. Los coches *fueron vendidos* por el Sr. Rivera.

   a. were repaired _____

   b. were driven   _____

   c. were washed   _____

4. Las flores *fueron escogidas* por Alicia.

   a. were watered _____

   b. were given   _____

   c. were bought _____

5. El espectáculo *fue visto* por muchos.

   a. was created   _____

   b. was done   _____

   c. was presented _____

6. La idea *fue entendida* por el presidente de la compañía.

   a. was rejected _____

   b. was received _____

   c. was suggested (sugerir) _____

7. La promesa *fue hecha* por los amigos.

   a. was broken   _____

   b. was given   _____

   c. was repeated _____

8. Los periódicos *fueron mandados* por un joven.

   a. were picked up _____

   b. were read   _____

   c. were written   _____

Rewrite the sentences. Change the impersonal *se* construction to a past participle expression. Use the verb *ser* in your answer, as well as the cues provided.

2.17   a.   Se abrió la puerta a las siete esta mañana. (el jefe)

   b.   Se venden las frutas en el mercado. (los granjeros)

   c.   Se escribe un buen libro. (Orzabal)

   d.   Se traduce el poema. (el profesor)

   e.   Se emplea una secretaria que habla francés. (la compañía internacional)

   f.   Se entienden las reglas. (todos los estudiantes)

   g.   Se cuenta la historia. (el anciano)

   h.   Se trae mucha comida. (los invitados)

   i.   Se pone la mesa. (la niña)

   j.   Se resuelven muchos misterios. (el detective)

LISTENING EXERCISES II

Exercise 1. The teacher is thinking about her class. She remembers in what order the students arrived at class today. Follow her thoughts and mark in what place each student came. [CD–E, Track 4]

Marina _____   MariCarmen y Beto _____

Chamo _____   Marcos _____

Carlos _____   Elisa _____

Manolo _____   Luisa _____

Guillermo _____   Antonio _____

Exercise 2. Listen carefully for the past participle in each sentence. Choose the infinitive which corresponds to each participle you hear. [CD–E, Track 5]

a. ser	pedir	ir
b. poder	poner	imponer
c. bailar	hablar	haber
d. ver	vestir	venir
e. pagar	jugar	tragar
f. pensar	peinar	poner
g. hacer	estar	abrir
h. venir	vender	ver
i. dormir	hacer	estar
j. sentir	volver	hacer

Exercise 3. Listen for the impersonal *se* expression in each sentence. Write the past participle for each verb given with *se*. [CD–E, Track 6]

a. _____   f. _____

b. _____   g. _____

c. _____   h. _____

d. _____   i. _____

e. _____   j. _____

III. THE PRESENT PERFECT TENSE

Now that you have learned the formation of the past participle, you are ready to study compound tenses (such as the present perfect and the pluperfect [past perfect] tenses). Each compound tense requires two parts to make up the conjugated verb form.

> compound tense form: helping verb + past participle

There is only one helping verb in Spanish: the verb *haber*. The tense of *haber* determines the compound tense that is being formed. For example, to form the **present perfect tense**, you use the **present** tense of *haber* plus the past participle; to form the **pluperfect tense**, you use the **imperfect** tense of *haber* plus the past participle; to form the **future perfect tense**, you use the **future** tense of *haber* plus the past participle; to form the **conditional perfect tense**, you use the **conditional** tense of *haber* plus the past participle.

The form of the past participle never changes when it is used as part of a compound tense verb expression. It uses the same form for all conjugated verbs in all the compound tenses, and it always ends in *-o*.

In this section, we are going to study the present perfect tense. To form this tense, you must first learn the present tense forms of *haber*.

	haber		
yo	**he**	nosotros	**hemos**
tú	**has**	vosotros	**habéis**
él, ella, Ud.	**ha**	ellos, ellas, Uds.	**han**

Examples:

he estudiado	I have studied	**hemos escrito**	we have written
has pedido	you have asked for	**habéis roto**	you have broken
ha dado	he has given	**han vuelto**	they have returned

Like English, the Spanish present perfect tense is used to describe an action that was completed in the past but still has a connection with the present.

 Identify the infinitive of the conjugated verb form in each sentence. Write your answer in the space provided.

3.1 a. No te has despertado temprano. _____

b. No me han llamado por muchas semanas. _____

c. ¿Ha leído un buen libro? _____

d. No he podido resolver el problema. _____

e. Hemos comprado muchas cosas allí. _____

f. ¿Quién ha puesto la mesa? _____

g. Me ha parecido extraño. _____

h. Nunca he conducido. _____

i. Han visto la película. _____

j. ¿Quién ha escrito esta carta? _____

▸ **Translate the following statements.**

3.2 a. He esperado el autobús. _____

b. He pensado mucho en este contrato. _____

c. Me he acostado temprano. _____

If each phrase was translated as "I have…", it is correct.

Try these other statements. Use the cues within each phrase to help you translate.

▸ **Translate the following statements.**

3.3 a. Tú has bailado mucho. _____

b. ¿Ha oído Ud. esta canción? _____

c. Ella no ha ido al museo tampoco. _____

d. Él ha dicho la verdad. _____

e. Nosotros no lo hemos creído. _____

f. ¿Han dormido bien ellos? _____

g. Ellas han hecho las maletas. _____

h. ¿Han estudiado español Uds.? _____

▸ **Use *has bailado*, the *tú* form of *bailar*, as a model to create the *tú* forms of these infinitives in the present perfect tense.**

3.4 a. lavar _____

b. buscar _____

c. beber _____

d. vender _____

e. ir _____

f. preferir _____

▶ **Which of those forms expresses...**

3.5 a. ...you have drunk? _____

    b. ...you have gone? _____

    c. ...you have washed? _____

    d. ...you have preferred? _____

    e. ...you have sold? _____

    f. ...you have looked (for)? _____

You already know that *no* is placed in front of the conjugated verb form to express negation. Because of this, you would express "You haven't washed" as *No has lavado*.

Remember that *has lavado* is ONE verb form, even though it is two words. Always keep the two parts of the verb form together.

▶ **Translate the following.**

3.6 a. you haven't looked (for) _____

    b. you haven't drunk _____

    c. you have not sold _____

    d. you haven't gone _____

    e. you have not preferred _____

▶ **Remembering to keep the two parts of the verb form together, make questions out of the forms.**

3.7 a. Have you washed? _____

    b. Have you looked (for)? _____

    c. Have you drunk? _____

    d. Have you sold? _____

    e. Have you gone? _____

    f. Have you preferred? _____

The above exercise should be simple. Just add question marks. Never separate a form of *haber* and the past participle.

Let's review one more aspect: the addition and placement of pronouns. For the sake of example, we'll use the direct object pronoun *lo* ("it"). Look at the model:

> *Lo has lavado* translates to "You have washed it."

Lo went in front of *has*, a form of *haber*. Your only option for object pronoun placement in a compound tense is always in front of the entire verb. Again, never separate a form of *haber* and the past participle.

▶ **Add *lo* to the rest of the sample phrases.**

3.8 a. You have looked for it. _____

b. You have drunk it. _____

c. You have sold it. _____

d. You have washed it. _____

Now you're ready to review the rest of the verb forms. Use the same sample infinitives for each subject to simplify this introduction. The *yo* form of *bailar* is *(yo) he bailado*.

▶ **Write the *yo* forms of these infinitives. Write the English translation of each form next to it.**

3.9 a. lavar _____

b. buscar _____

c. beber _____

d. vender _____

e. ir _____

f. preferir _____

▶ **Express the following.**

3.10 a. I haven't washed it. _____

b. I haven't looked for it. _____

c. Haven't I drunk it? _____

d. I have sold it. _____

e. I haven't gone there. _____

▶ **Continue with the *él/ella/Ud.* forms. Write the English translation of each form next to it.**

Example: cantar   *Él/Ella/Ud.* ha cantado   He/She has sung. / You have sung.

3.11   a.   lavar _____

b.   buscar _____

c.   beber _____

d.   vender _____

e.   ir _____

f.   preferir _____

▶ **Express the following.**

3.12   a.   She hasn't washed it. _____

b.   You have not looked for it. _____

c.   He hasn't drunk it. _____

d.   Has he sold it? _____

e.   She hasn't preferred it. _____

▶ **Express the following.**

3.13   a.   Haven't we washed it? _____

b.   We have not looked for it. _____

c.   Have we drunk it? _____

d.   We haven't sold it. _____

e.   We have not gone there. _____

f.   We haven't preferred it. _____

▶ **Express the following using the *ellos/ellas/Uds.* verb form each time.**

Example: cantar
   ellos/ellas/Uds. han cantado

3.14   a.   lavar _____

b.   buscar _____

c.   beber _____

d.   vender _____

e. ir _____

f. preferir _____

g. They haven't washed it. _____

h. Have they looked for it? _____

i. Haven't you drunk it? _____

j. You have not sold it. _____

k. You haven't gone there. _____

l. They haven't preferred it. _____

Review these forms. Summarize the present-tense forms of *haber* by writing them in the chart below.

3.15 **haber**—to have

a. yo	d. nosotros
b. tú	e. vosotros **habéis**
c. él, ella, Ud.	f. ellos, ellas, Uds.

Although *haber* means *to have*, its role is primarily that of a helping verb. It is not used to show possession. It is not interchangeable with *tener*.

To form the present perfect tense, a past participle must follow the form of *haber*. To review: the past participle of an AR verb is formed by dropping the -*ar* and adding -*ado*; the past participle of an ER or IR verb is formed by dropping the -*er* or -*ir* and adding -*ido*.

Fill in the charts with the present perfect forms of the infinitives given.

3.16 **ser**—to be

a. yo	d. nosotros
b. tú	e. vosotros **habéis sido**
c. él, ella, Ud.	f. ellos, ellas, Uds.

To review: *hemos sido* expresses "we have been," *ha sido* expresses "he has been," and *he sido* translates as "I have been."

3.17 **acostarse** —to go to bed

a. yo	d. nosotros
b. tú	e. vosotros **os habéis acostado**
c. él, ella, Ud.	f. ellos, ellas, Uds.

To review: "they have gone to bed" translates as *se han acostado*, "you have gone to bed" translates as *te has (Ud. se ha) acostado*, and "I have gone to bed" translates as *me he acostado*.

3.18 **escribir**—to write

a. yo	d. nosotros
b. tú	e. vosotros **habéis escrito**
c. él, ella, Ud.	f. ellos, ellas, Uds.

To review: "I have written" translates as *he escrito*, "all of you have written" translates as *Uds. han escrito*, and "we have written" translates as *hemos escrito*.

Choose the present perfect form that agrees with the given subject.

3.19 1. Ud. y mis parientes _____
   a. han descubierto
   b. ha descubierto
   c. has descubierto

2. el jefe y yo _____
   a. han leído
   b. hemos leído
   c. he leído

3. el señor _____
   a. he vuelto
   b. han vuelto
   c. ha vuelto

4. mi equipo _____
   a. ha ganado
   b. han ganado
   c. hemos ganado

43

5. tú _____
   a. ha hecho
   b. han hecho
   c. has hecho

6. Manolo y su padre _____
   a. has estado
   b. ha estado
   c. han estado

7. Ud. _____
   a. ha mostrado
   b. has mostrado
   c. han mostrado

8. mi mejor amiga _____
   a. he querido
   b. ha querido
   c. han querido

9. tu hermano y yo _____
   a. han salido
   b. hemos salido
   c. ha salido

10. el grupo de jóvenes _____
    a. han creado
    b. hemos creado
    c. ha creado

▶ **Change the given present perfect form to agree with the new subjects for each group.**

3.20 1. No has visto nunca este evento.
   a. Tomás no lo _____ nunca.
   b. Virginia y yo lo _____ ya.
   c. Ustedes lo _____ muchas veces.
   d. ¿Cuándo lo _____ tú?

2. He hecho un pastel de manzana para la cena.
   a. Mi hermano _____ una ensalada.
   b. Mis padres _____ muchos panecillos.
   c. ¿Por qué no _____ tú nada?
   d. Nosotros siempre _____ la cena juntos.

3. ¿Cómo ha estado Ud.?
   a. Yo _____ muy bien, gracias.
   b. Y tú, ¿cómo _____?
   c. Desgraciadamente, Paco _____ muy mal.
   d. Mis abuelos _____ bien, más o menos.

4. ¿Ya se han levantado Uds.?
   a. Ellas no _____ .
   b. Ni nosotros _____ tampoco.
   c. Pero tú siempre _____ temprano.
   d. Mi hermano nunca _____ temprano.

5. Han resuelto el problema de matemáticas.
   a. El profesor _____ el problema conmigo.
   b. Los estudiantes _____ el problema juntos.
   c. Sacas malas notas porque no _____ muchos problemas.
   d. Soy inteligente. _____ todos los problemas por mí mismo.

SPANISH II LIFEPAC TEST UNIT 8

Name _____

Date _____

Score _____

96 / 120

1. Fill in the space provided in each sentence with a past participle of one of the infinitives listed. Not all the infinitives will be used. (1 pt. each)

Infinitives			
ser	cubrir	hacer	recomendar
tener	cerrar	mantener	morir
ver	cortar	jugar	llenar
escribir	comprar	trabajar	decir

a. El coche siempre funciona. Es bien _____ .

b. El libro es antiguo. Fue _____ hace muchos años.

c. La camisa es nueva. Fue _____ ayer.

d. Vamos a emplear a esa mujer. Es _____ por el presidente de la compañía.

e. Las flores no están vivos. Están _____ .

f. No necesitamos gasolina. El tanque fue _____ esta mañana.

g. El pelo parece terrible. El peluquero lo ha _____ mal.

h. No podemos salir. La puerta está _____ con llave.

i. La niña que desapareció (disappeared) fue _____ por muchas personas esta mañana.

j. No tengo frío. Estoy _____ de una manta.

2. Circle the letter of the correct translation of each present perfect form. (1 pt. each)

1. hemos partido
    a. we have left
    b. they have left
    c. we were leaving

2. has tenido
    a. you had (friendly)
    b. you have had (friendly)
    c. you have had (formal)

3. han sufrido
    a. they had suffered
    b. we have suffered
    c. they have suffered

4. he podido
    a. I have been able
    b. I was able
    c. I had been able

5. ¿Lo ha bebido?
   a. Has he drunk it?
   b. He hasn't drunk it?
   c. He drank it?

6. hemos descrito
   a. we have written
   b. we have described
   c. we had written

7. No se lo han quitado.
   a. They have taken it off.
   b. Have they taken it off?
   c. They haven't taken it off.

8. has ido
   a. you've gone
   b. all of you have gone
   c. they have gone

9. ha atraído
   a. she has brought
   b. I have attracted
   c. he has attracted

10. hemos roto
    a. we haven't broken
    b. they have broken
    c. we have broken

3. **Change each present perfect form given to agree with the new subject.** (1 pt. each)

   a. Rosita lo ha cubierto. Y yo lo _____ .
   b. La clase los ha visto. Y tú los _____ .
   c. Tú la has cambiado. Y tú y yo la _____ .
   d. No me he vestido. Y nuestros padres no _____ .
   e. ¿Quién ha corrido? ¿Quiénes _____ ?
   f. Nos hemos despertado. Y la Sra. Lorca _____ .
   g. Lo has dicho. Y yo lo _____ .
   h. No las han pedido. Y Ud. no las _____ .
   i. Yo he vivido allí. Y nosotros _____ allí.
   j. El partido ha terminado. Y la práctica _____ .

4. **Change the infinitives given to agree with the person indicated in each sentence. Use the present perfect tense.** (1 pt. each)

   a. Gracias, yo _____ antes. (comer)
   b. El estudiante no _____ a esa lección. (asistir)
   c. Me _____ todas las artes. (gustar)
   d. Sus padres no _____ nada de sus problemas en la escuela. (oír)
   e. Mi familia _____ paseos en coche muchas veces. (dar)
   f. Jorge y su amigo _____ las llaves para el coche. (perder)
   g. Muchas veces esa señorita _____ temprano. (salir)
   h. Mi hermanito se siente orgulloso. _____ la mesa solo. (poner)
   i. ¿Por qué no _____ Uds. esa novela? Porque no nos interesa. (leer)
   j. Tú no _____ el secreto a Manolo, ¿verdad? (decir)

5. **Write the *tú* and *Uds.* forms of the *pluperfect tense* for each given infinitive.** (1 pt. each answer)

	tú	Uds.
a. ser		
b. pronunciar		
c. abrir		
d. cuidar		
e. divertirse		
f. acabar		
g. leer		
h. pescar		
i. no maquillarse		
j. dormir		

6. **The following verb forms are written in a variety of forms and tenses. Change each one to the same form of the present perfect tense.** (1 pt. each)

a. jugaste _____ i. leías _____

b. quieren _____ j. estoy dando _____

c. veíamos _____ k. te diviertes _____

d. muestro _____ l. dormimos _____

e. eres _____ m. abre _____

f. se pondrá _____ n. conozco _____

g. no piensan _____ o. dijimos _____

h. fuimos _____

7. **Complete this activity in the same manner as the previous one, except this time write the verb forms in the pluperfect tense.** (1 pt. each)

a. están saliendo _____ i. tienen _____

b. anduviste _____ j. describirás _____

c. di _____ k. hizo _____

d. hablamos _____ l. costarían _____

e. sabrían _____ m. sigues _____

f. corrió _____ n. rompes _____

g. saqué _____ o. conversamos _____

h. no creemos _____

8. **Read and translate the following story.** (10 pts.)

El día empezó temprano. Yo había oído el ladrar (the barking) de mi perro, Huesito, cuando estaba todavía en la cama. Me levanté para dejarlo salir. Hacía mucho frío. Abrí la puerta y Huesito salió muy de prisa. Yo lo seguí hasta el jardín. De repente, creí que había oído un «clic» extraño cuando cerró la puerta. Tenía razón. ¡La puerta se había cerrado con llave automáticamente! ¡Estaba todavía fuera de la casa! (¡Y yo llevaba sólo los pijamas!) Estaba a punto de pánico cuando recordé...

_____
_____
_____
_____
_____
_____
_____

9. **Write ten (10) more complete Spanish sentences to complete the story you just translated.**
(2 pts. each sentence)

_____
_____
_____
_____
_____
_____
_____
_____
_____
_____
_____
_____
_____

✓ Adult check _____
            Initial   Date

Translate the forms for each group into Spanish.

3.21 1. morirse
   a. (It) has died. _____
   b. They have died. _____
   c. She has died. _____

2. imprimir
   a. The company has printed it. _____
   b. The students have printed it. _____
   c. We haven't printed it. _____

3. caerse
   a. Beto has fallen down. _____
   b. I've fallen down. _____
   c. Have they fallen down? _____

4. jugar
   a. We've played tennis. _____
   b. You (Tú) haven't played tennis. _____
   c. When has your family played tennis? _____

5. vestirse
   a. She has gotten dressed. _____
   b. I haven't gotten dressed. _____
   c. They have gotten dressed. _____

6. romper
   a. I've broken the glass. _____
   b. My friend has broken the glass. _____
   c. All of you have broken the glass. _____

7. poder
   a. Have you (tú) been able to study? _____
   b. We haven't been able to study. _____
   c. The students have been able to study. _____

8. salir
   a. I have gone out tonight. _____
   b. When has your sister gone out? _____
   c. We haven't gone out tonight. _____

9. pagar
   a. You (Tú) haven't paid the bill. _____
   b. He has paid the bill. _____
   c. Have we paid the bill? _____

10. dar
   a. Luisa and Enrique have given it to me. _____
   b. You and I have given it to them. _____
   c. Have you (formal) given it to him? _____

Use a present perfect expression to describe what just happened to each person.

3.22 a. El bebé _____.   b. El fotógrafo _____ un retrato.

c. Los maridos _____ las llaves.   d. Nosotros _____.

e. Yo _____ muchos kilómetros.   f. El Sr. Guzmán _____ _____.

g. Uds. _____ la ventana.   h. Alejandro _____ el libro a la biblioteca.

46

i. Tú _____ un regalo grande.

j. El testigo _____ la verdad.

> You have already learned that the phrase *acabar + de + infinitive* means *to have just (done something)*. Express the same idea with the present perfect tense by changing the *acabar de* expressions to the equivalent of the present perfect tense.

3.23
a. Acabamos de perder otra vez.

_____ otra vez recientemente.

b. Acabas de decir una mentira.

_____ una mentira recientemente.

c. Acabo de escribir un ensayo.

_____ un ensayo recientemente.

d. Elena acaba de ir de vacaciones.

Elena _____ de vacaciones recientemente.

e. Los jóvenes acaban de traer las bebidas.

Los jóvenes _____ las bebidas recientemente.

f. Acabo de poner esa caja allá.

_____ esa caja allá recientemente.

g. ¿Acabas de darle de comer al perro?

¿Le _____ de comer al perro recientemente?

h. Tus amigos acaban de obtener un coche.

Tus amigos _____ un coche recientemente.

i. Acabamos de salir de la casa.

_____ de la casa recientemente.

j. Ud. acaba de devolver dos libros a la biblioteca.

Ud. _____ dos libros a la biblioteca recientemente.

Answer the following questions in complete Spanish sentences. Use a present perfect verb form in each of your responses.

3.24   a.   ¿Para qué clase has escrito un ensayo importante?
_____

b.   ¿No ha oído Ud. nunca la música latina?
_____

c.   ¿Quién te ha dado un regalo especial?
_____

d.   ¿Cuándo has viajado muy lejos de casa?
_____

e.   ¿Qué te ha gustado hacer en el invierno?
_____

f.   ¿Cómo te has sentido hoy?
_____

g.   ¿Ha almorzado tu mejor amigo contigo recientemente?
_____

h.   ¿Quién ha sacado las mejores notas de tu clase?
_____

i.   ¿Dónde has trabajado?
_____

j.   ¿Cuándo han asistido Uds. a una gran fiesta?
_____

Read the note and answer the questions.

Querida mamá:

He ido a la casa de Consuelo. He comido el bocadillo que me dejaste. ¡Muchas gracias! Como me has pedido, le he dado de comer al gato. También he lavado los platos. Chamo no ha vuelto del partido. Carlos no ha sacado la basura a la calle. Laura y yo hemos conversado un poquito; ya sabemos que tenemos que regresar para la cena.

Hasta esta noche.

Mil besos,

Beto

3.25
1. Carlos es _____ .
   a. un padre
   b. un hijo
   c. el marido
2. El animal doméstico de la casa es _____ .
   a. un gato
   b. Chamo
   c. un perro
3. Los hijos tienen que regresar aproximadamente para _____ .
   a. el mediodía
   b. las seis de la noche
   c. las nueve de la noche
4. Beto escribe la carta a _____ .
   a. Chamo
   b. Laura
   c. su madre
5. Al regresar a casa, Beto tiene _____ .
   a. sed
   b. hambre
   c. sueño

 Carefully read the note below and answer the questions that follow.

Alonso:

¿Dónde has estado? Te he esperado durante treinta minutos. Hemos hablado de esto a la biblioteca. ¿Te has olvidado? Ya no puedo esperar; he prometido a mi hermanita que iremos al parque esta tarde. Son las dos ahora; he planeado regresar a casa a las cuatro. Llámame.

Consuelo

3.26
1. Consuelo debe estar _____ .
   a. paciente
   b. irritada
   c. contenta
2. Consuelo llegó a la casa de Alonso a _____ .
   a. la una y media
   b. las dos
   c. las dos y media
3. Consuelo y Alonso probablemente necesitan _____ .
   a. comer
   b. dar un paseo
   c. hacer una tarea

4. Después de escribir la carta, Consuelo ____ .
   a. esperó
   b. fue a la biblioteca
   c. fue al parque

5. Alonso debe llamarla después de ____ .
   a. las dos
   b. la una y media
   c. las cuatro

▶ **Change the following verb forms to the present perfect tense, keeping the same subject.**

3.27
a. bailamos _____
b. vivieron _____
c. vendrías _____
d. jugué _____
e. fueron _____
f. veíamos _____
g. hizo _____
h. piden _____
i. se acostará _____
j. querría _____
k. pudiste _____
l. devolvemos _____
m. escribías _____
n. leyeron _____
o. estudio _____

▶ **Write a letter of recommendation.**

3.28 Imagine that you have been asked to write a letter of recommendation in Spanish for a friend, who has been nominated for an award. Write at least ten complete sentences detailing the reasons why your friend deserves an achievement award. Use the present perfect tense to explain what your friend has done to deserve it.

_____
_____
_____
_____
_____
_____
_____
_____
_____
_____
_____
_____
_____

✓ Adult check _____
                    Initial   Date

LISTENING EXERCISES III

Exercise 1. Listen carefully to the following English sentences. Decide if the Spanish equivalent of that sentence would require a *present perfect* verb form, a present tense form of *tener que + infinitive*, or a present tense form of *tener* alone. Write your choice in the space provided. Write *present perfect*, *tener que*, or *tener*. [CD–E, Track 7]

a. _____
b. _____
c. _____
d. _____
e. _____
f. _____
g. _____
h. _____
i. _____
j. _____

Exercise 2. Listen carefully for the present perfect verb form of each Spanish sentence. Circle the infinitive of the present perfect verb form given. [CD–E, Track 8]

1. a. haber
   b. preparar
   c. parar

2. a. ir
   b. ver
   c. pedir

3. a. poder
   b. pagar
   c. ver

4. a. comer
   b. ser
   c. crear

5. a. dar
   b. vestirse
   c. haber

6. a. ser
   b. poder
   c. poner

7. a. estar
   b. dar
   c. encontrar

8. a. ganar
   b. hacer
   c. parecer

9. a. devolver
   b. ir
   c. volver

10. a. llover
    b. poder
    c. ayudar

51

Exercise 3. Each of the following sentences contains an *acabar de* + *infinitive* expression. After you hear each sentence twice, rewrite just the main verb with the corresponding present perfect verb form. [CD–E, Track 9]

a. _____
b. _____
c. _____
d. _____
e. _____
f. _____
g. _____
h. _____
i. _____
j. _____

IV. THE PLUPERFECT TENSE

> Nunca **he viajado** a Europa, pero para la edad de nueve años, **había viajado** al Canadá.
>
> **He leído** esta novela; pero nunca **había leído** esa novela antes.
>
> Todavía no **he oído** nada de ella; para ayer no **había oído** mucho de él tampoco.

 Read the above statements. You recognize the first forms in each phrase as the present perfect tense. The second form in each sentence is the pluperfect tense. Compare the two tenses. Write the pairs of forms below.

4.1   a. _____

       b. _____

       c. _____

They are similar, because **each tense uses the past participle** *(viajado, leído, oído)*. The progression to the pluperfect tense is natural after the present perfect, because each tense utilizes the past participle. Hence, their meanings are very similar as well. Let's look at these statements again.

> Nunca **he viajado** a Europa, pero para la edad de nueve años, **había viajado** al Canadá.
> *I have never traveled to Europe, but by the age of nine, I had traveled to Canada.*
>
> **He leído** esta novela; pero nunca **había leído** esa novela antes.
> *I have read this novel, but I had never read that novel before.*
>
> Todavía no **he oído** nada de ella; para ayer no **había oído** mucho de él tampoco.
> *I still haven't heard from her; by yesterday I hadn't heard much from him either.*

We already know the present perfect form *he viajado* translates as "I have traveled." The pluperfect form of this same verb would be *había viajado,* and it translates as "I had traveled."

The pluperfect verb tense is often used to express a past action prior to another past action or a past point in time.

> **Ya habíamos terminado la tarea cuando Roberto nos encontró en la biblioteca ayer.**
> We had already finished the homework when Robert met us in the library yesterday.
>
> **Mis amigos ya habían cenado antes de ir al cine anoche.**
> My friends had already had dinner before going to the movies last night.

The same rules about the position of object pronouns and negative words and phrases apply to the pluperfect tense as to the present perfect tense. Never put object pronouns or negatives between the two parts of the compound tense (between the helping verb and the past participle).

> **Ya no la habíamos terminado cuando Roberto nos encontró en la biblioteca ayer.**
> We had not already finished it *(la tarea)* when Robert met us in the library yesterday.

As you have already learned, the present perfect tense is formed by using the present tense of *haber* + the past participle. In the same manner, the pluperfect tense is formed by using the imperfect tense of *haber* + the past participle. Like the present perfect tense, the past participle used in the pluperfect tense never changes.

The following chart shows the imperfect tense forms of *haber*.

haber—to have

yo **había**	nosotros **habíamos**
tú **habías**	vosotros **habíais**
él, ella, Ud. **había**	ellos, ellas, Uds. **habían**

 Study the charts. Translate the verb forms.

4.2 1. **leer**—to read

a. yo	**había leído**	d. nosotros	**habíamos leído**
b. tú	**habías leído**	e. vosotros	**habíais leído**
c. él, ella, Ud.	**había leído**	f. ellos, ellas, Uds.	**habían leído**

2. **viajar**—to travel

a. yo	**había viajado**	d. nosotros	**habíamos viajado**
b. tú	**habías viajado**	e. vosotros	**habíais viajado**
c. él, ella, Ud.	**había viajado**	f. ellos, ellas, Uds.	**habían viajado**

3. **oír**—to hear

a. yo	**había oído**	d. nosotros	**habíamos oído**
b. tú	**habías oído**	e. vosotros	**habíais oído**
c. él, ella, Ud.	**había oído**	f. ellos, ellas, Uds.	**habían oído**

✔ Adult check _____
　　　　　　　　　　　　 Initial　　　　　　　　　　　　　　Date

▶ **Write the English translation of these forms of the pluperfect tense.**

4.3　a.　tú lo habías estudiado _____

　　 b.　nosotros habíamos comido _____

　　 c.　ellos habían escrito _____

　　 d.　yo había vivido _____

　　 e.　Uds. habían comprendido _____

　　 f.　yo había pagado _____

　　 g.　ella había cantado _____

　　 h.　Ud. las había vendido _____

　　 i.　nosotros habíamos ido _____

　　 j.　me había gustado eso _____

Keeping in mind that the pluperfect tense is similar in structure to the present perfect, write the negative of each of the verb phrases from Exercise 4.3. The first one has been done for you.

4.4 a. _____tú no lo habías estudiado_____
     b. _____
     c. _____
     d. _____
     e. _____
     f. _____
     g. _____
     h. _____
     i. _____
     j. _____

Translate the above phrases into English.

4.5 a. _____
     b. _____
     c. _____
     d. _____
     e. _____
     f. _____
     g. _____
     h. _____
     i. _____
     j. _____

Translate the following.

4.6 a. ¿Habíamos comido la fruta? _____
     b. ¿Se la habían escrito ellos? _____
     c. ¿No había vivido yo allí? _____
     d. ¿Lo habían comprendido Uds.? _____
     e. ¿Ya no había pagado la cuenta yo? _____

f. ¿No había bailado ella? _____

g. ¿No lo había vendido Ud.? _____

h. ¿Habíamos ido a la fiesta? _____

i. ¿No te había gustado el regalo? _____

j. ¿Habías roto la ventana? _____

Use the original charts as a guide to fill in the *pluperfect* forms of these infinitives.

4.7 **cortar**—to cut

a. yo	d. nosotros
b. tú	vosotros **habíais cortado**
c. él, ella, Ud.	e. ellos, ellas, Uds.

4.8 **sufrir**—to suffer

a. yo	d. nosotros
b. tú	vosotros **habíais sufrido**
c. él, ella, Ud.	e. ellos, ellas, Uds.

4.9   **perder**—to lose

a. yo	d. nosotros
b. tú	vosotros **habíais perdido**
c. él, ella, Ud.	e. ellos, ellas, Uds.

4.10   **morir**—to die

a. yo	d. nosotros
b. tú	vosotros **habíais muerto**
c. él, ella, Ud.	e. ellos, ellas, Uds.

4.11   **despertarse**—to wake up

a. yo	d. nosotros
b. tú	vosotros **os habíais despertado**
c. él, ella, Ud.	e. ellos, ellas, Uds.

Write the indicated pluperfect form of the infinitive given.

4.12
a. marcharse (tú) _____
b. ir (ellos) _____
c. vestirse (nosotros) _____
d. no abrir (yo) _____
e. sacar (Uds.) _____
f. querer (ella) _____
g. no pensar (la familia) _____
h. seguir (tú y yo) _____
i. concluir (el profesor) _____
j. romper (los atletas) _____
k. dar (Elena) _____
l. no tener (mis padres) _____
m. escribir (Ud. y su novio) _____
n. estar (Chamo, Nacho, Julieta y Vilma) _____
o. salir (mi familia y yo) _____

Complete each sentence with the appropriate pluperfect form of the infinitive given.

4.13
a. ¡Qué extraño! Yo nunca _____ tal cosa antes de ayer. (ver)

b. Marisol no _____ hacer la cena antes del partido ayer. (prometer)

c. ¿Ya _____ tú antes de nuestra llegada ayer? (almorzar)

d. Uds. no _____ más de tres kilómetros cuando reventó (burst) la llanta. (viajar)

e. Anita ya no _____ antes de los otros ayer. (levantarse)

f. De repente (Suddenly) me di cuenta (I realized) que yo _____ la billetera. (perder)

g. Las niñas le confesaron a la policía que no le _____ la verdad el martes pasado. (decir)

h. Fuimos al lugar donde los soldados _____ el año pasado. (morir)

i. Jorge y su novia ya _____ al espectáculo anoche cuando los vimos en el café. (asistir)

j. Mi hermano y yo ya _____ a caballo en este bosque cuando nuestros padres llegaron en casa. (montar)

The *yo* forms of the pluperfect tense have been given. Change those forms to the *tú* and *nosotros* forms of the pluperfect tense.

4.14

	tú	nosotros
a. había jugado		
b. me había presentado		
c. no había oído		
d. había recogido		
e. había desayunado		
f. había entretenido		
g. había descubierto		
h. había deshecho		
i. había resuelto		
j. había trabajado		

Decide how each person got into this situation by reading the circumstances in parentheses. Express what had previously happened in that situation by writing affirmative or negative statements in the pluperfect tense. Use the cues provided in your answers. The first one has been done for you.

4.15 a. Alonso tenía hambre. (comer/trabajar mucho) *Alonso no había comido. Había trabajado mucho.*

b. Yo saqué malas notas en el examen. (mirar la televisión/estudiar)
_____

c. Mi familia y yo nos perdimos. (seguir el mapa/doblar en la calle incorrecta)
_____

d. No fuiste a la fiesta. (estar enferma/acostarse temprano)
_____

e. Tu equipo no ganó el campeonato. (jugar mal/practicar bien)

f. Sus padres se enojaron con Ud. (tener cuidado/romper el vaso)

g. Yo tenía dolor de cabeza. (tomar aspirina/ponerse las gafas)

h. Recibió el premio Nobel. (hacer mucha investigación/ayudar a la raza humana)

i. Me gradué de la universidad. (asistir a muchas fiestas/dedicarse a los estudios)

j. Me puso una multa por el accidente (conducir muy rápidamente/prestar atención)

Translate these sentences into English.

4.16
a. Ya había empezado a nevar cuando decidieron salir.

b. Imprimieron tu artículo ayer, pero ya habían impreso el mío la semana pasada.

c. ¿Había prestado atención en clase Luisa antes de recibir la mala nota en matemáticas?

d. ¿Quién te había ayudado a comprender las diferencias entre el pretérito y el imperfecto antes de la clase de español ayer?

e. Teníamos hambre porque no habíamos desayunado mucho.

Translate these sentences into Spanish.

4.17 a. My friend told me that our team had already lost the game when I arrived.

b. Had you (friendly) already gone shopping before meeting me (reunirse con) for lunch yesterday?

c. They told me they had opened the gates at 8:00 this morning.

d. We had already gotten the boarding passes when they cancelled (cancelar) the flight.

e. Anita had already left when Josefina arrived.

f. Did all of you go to the house where your grandparents had died last year?

g. Had you (friendly) already bought a gift for your mother before losing your purse yesterday?

h. I had already thought a lot about my future career before graduation from high school last week.

i. We had already visited our aunt in the hospital when we found out that our uncle had crashed into a tree.

j. I had already told the truth to my parents when the policeman arrived.

Complete the following composition.

4.18 Think back five years ago. How old were you? Where had you been living? Had you attended the school or class you are in now? Did you have the same friends you have now? On a separate sheet of paper, write a composition of ten complete sentences in Spanish. Use the pluperfect, preterit, and imperfect tenses to describe your life at that time.

✓ Adult check _____
                             Initial   Date

LISTENING EXERCISES IV

Exercise 1. Listen carefully to the verb forms in each sentence. Decide if you hear the present perfect, the pluperfect, or the present tense. Name the tense of your choice in the space provided. [CD–E, Track 10]

a. _____
b. _____
c. _____
d. _____
e. _____
f. _____
g. _____
h. _____
i. _____
j. _____

Exercise 2. Listen carefully for the preterit or imperfect verb form in each statement. Write the corresponding *pluperfect* verb form of that same infinitive in the space provided for each answer. [CD–E, Track 11]

a. _____
b. _____
c. _____
d. _____
e. _____
f. _____
g. _____
h. _____
i. _____
j. _____

Exercise 3. **Answer the following questions in complete Spanish sentences. Use the same verb tense in your answer as in the question.** [CD–E, Track 12]

a. _____

b. _____

c. _____

d. _____

e. _____

Review the material in this section in preparation for the Self Test. This Self Test will check your mastery of this particular section as well as your knowledge of the previous sections.

SELF TEST 2–4

4.01 For each Spanish infinitive, state the past participle of that infinitive and then give its English meaning. (1 pt. each)

		Past Participle	Meaning of Past Participle
a.	jugar		
b.	comprender		
c.	ser		
d.	ver		
e.	dar		
f.	resolver		
g.	vivir		
h.	estudiar		
i.	cubrir		
j.	escribir		
k.	correr		
l.	morir		
m.	creer		
n.	secar		
o.	preferir		

4.02 Using a form of the verb *estar*, give a past participle used as an adjective to describe the pictures. Choose from the list of infinitives below. Use each verb once only. (1 pt. each)

> desilusionar   sentar   apagar   abrir
> romper   destruir   quemar   cerrar

 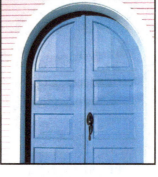  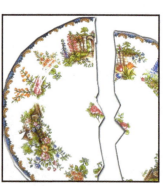

a. _____   b. _____   c. _____   d. _____

e. _____   f. _____   g. _____   h. _____

4.03 **Use the given infinitive to translate each phrase into Spanish. Be careful to choose the correct verb tense each time.** (1 pt. each)

1. sentirse
   a. you (friendly) have felt _____
   b. we haven't felt _____
   c. they had felt _____

2. charlar
   a. I had chatted _____
   b. they haven't chatted _____
   c. you (friendly) had chatted _____

3. poner
   a. they had put _____
   b. he had put _____
   c. I haven't put _____

4. decir
   a. you (friendly) haven't told _____
   b. she has told _____
   c. they hadn't told _____

5. repetir
   a. he had repeated _____
   b. I have repeated _____
   c. you (friendly) haven't repeated _____

6. ir
   a. we had gone _____
   b. he had gone _____
   c. she and I have gone _____

7. volver
   a. you (friendly) had returned _____
   b. I have returned _____
   c. Elisa has returned _____

4.04 Complete the first column of the chart with the correct present perfect form of the infinitive given. Complete the second column with the corresponding pluperfect form. (1 pt. each)

		Present Perfect	Pluperfect
a.	estar (Uds.)		
b.	ser (tú)		
c.	vestirse (nosotros)		
d.	acostarse (tú)		
e.	imprimir (la fábrica)		
f.	hacer (yo)		
g.	encender (la lámpara)		
h.	salir (los jóvenes)		
i.	saber (yo)		
j.	casarse (los novios)		

4.05 Rewrite these present tense sentences in the pluperfect tense. (1 pt. each)

a. Visitan el lugar donde murió su abuela.
   Visitaron el lugar donde _____ su abuela.

b. No le gusta leer.
   Ya no le _____ leer para la edad de seis años.

c. ¿Puedes llamarla por teléfono?
   ¿Ya _____ llamarla por teléfono antes de su llegada esta mañana?

d. Le hablo bien el español a mi familia.
   Ya le _____ bien el español a mi familia para la edad de cinco años.

e. Nosotros nadamos en el lago.
   Nosotros ya _____ en el lago antes de la tormenta ayer.

f. El viernes devuelves las revistas a la biblioteca porque has terminado de leerlas.
   El viernes devolviste las revistas a la biblioteca porque _____ de leerlas.

g. Los estudiantes tienen que escoger un buen tema para la composición.
   Los estudiantes ya _____ que escoger un buen tema para la composición antes del comienzo de la clase ayer.

h. Pones la mesa para el almuerzo.
   Ya _____ la mesa para el almuerzo antes de preparar la comida.

i. La madre de Luis planta rosas en el jardín.
    La madre de Luis ya _____ rosas en el jardín antes de plantar otras flores.

j. ¿Qué haces para el desayuno?
    ¿Qué _____ para el desayuno antes de mi llegada?

4.06 **Everyone, at times, has not fulfilled certain responsibilities for any number of reasons. Use the present perfect tense in the first phrase to describe what the given subject has not done. Use the pluperfect tense in the second phrase to offer an excuse, saying what had occurred instead.** (2 pts. each)

a. lavar los platos / cortarse la mano (Chela) _____

b. darle de comer al perro / terminar la tarea (el hijo de Raúl) _____

c. devolver el libro a la biblioteca (tú) / reventarse (burst) (la llanta de la bicicleta) _____

d. escribir la tarea / tener dolor de cabeza (el estudiante) _____

e. llamarte / hacer mucho trabajo en casa (yo) _____

f. servir el café / no lavar las tazas (los primos) _____

g. cortar la hierba / no comprar gasolina (tu hermano mayor) _____

h. leer la novela / ver un programa interesante en la televisión (Rita y su amiga) _____

i. no revisar el artículo / no tener tiempo (la editora) _____

j. no reparar mi coche / ir al hospital con su esposa (el mecánico) _____

4.07 Express the following phrases in Spanish. Use an ordinal number in each of your responses.
(1 pt. each)

a. the first day _____

b. the eighth person _____

c. the sixth time (vez) _____

d. the third class _____

e. the ninth problem _____

f. the tenth finger _____

g. the fourth movie _____

h. the fifth exam _____

i. the second sister _____

j. the first class _____

k. the seventh day _____

l. the third car _____

103 / 129

Score _____

Adult check _____
                     Initial   Date

V. REVIEW OF UNIT SEVEN

▶ **Fill in the blanks with the correct future tense form of the regular infinitives given.**

5.1 a. ¿_____ tus padres la cena hoy? (cocinar)

   b. El próximo mes yo _____ una novela larga. (leer)

   c. ¿Cuándo _____ la tristeza? (terminar)

   d. Ya sé que los niños no _____ la verdad. (entender)

   e. Pues, Consuelo y yo _____ un pastel. (traer)

   f. Yo _____ en quince años. (jubilarse)

   g. Es imposible. Mis padres no lo _____ nunca. (permitir)

   h. Tú _____ a la reunión a las ocho. (asistir)

   i. ¿Quién nos _____ ? (hablar)

   j. ¿Qué _____ tú? (pedir)

▶ **Continue this exercise with the following irregular infinitives.**

5.2 a. ¿A qué hora _____ Uds.? (venir)

   b. Desafortunadamente, tú _____ que sentarte al fondo del coche. (tener)

   c. Estoy seguro de que nadie _____ lo que pasó. (saber)

   d. Mis hijos _____ las camas mañana. (hacer)

   e. Yo le _____ a mi madre que Ud. la llamó. (decir)

   f. Tú _____ estudiar conmigo, ¿no? (querer)

   g. Mis amigos y yo _____ pronto. (salir)

   h. ¿Dónde _____ ellos los impermeables? (poner)

   i. En treinta años, ¿cuánto _____ estas pinturas? (valer)

   j. Si no duerme bien, ella _____ dolor de cabeza. (tener)

▶ **The following sentences use the expression *ir + a + infinitive* or the present tense to describe future events. Rewrite them, using an equivalent form of the future tense.**

5.3 a. Mis nietos van a visitar me. _____

   b. ¿Qué pides? _____

71

c. El sábado Patricia tiene cinco años. _____

d. No vamos a jugar al fútbol mañana. _____

e. Los jóvenes se levantan temprano mañana. _____

f. Piensas decir la verdad. _____

g. No cuesta mucho la chaqueta. _____

h. Voy a ponerme el traje nuevo. _____

i. Vamos a España el verano que viene. _____

j. La secretaria va a archivar las copias. _____

Translate the phrases into Spanish twice. Use *ir + a + infinitive* for your first response and the future tense for your second.

5.4 1. Who (is going to) will come tomorrow?

a. _____

b. _____

2. My parents (aren't going to) will not be there.

a. _____

b. _____

3. You (are going to) will see him soon.

a. _____

b. _____

4. We (aren't going to) won't write the letter.

a. _____

b. _____

5. What time (is it going to) will it be?

a. _____

b. _____

6. It (is going to) will be hot outside tomorrow.

a. _____

b. _____

7. They (are going to) will lose the game.

a. _____

b. _____

8. Won't you (Aren't you going to) help me?

   a. _____

   b. _____

9. We (aren't going to) won't want it (lo).

   a. _____

   b. _____

10. Will she (Is she going to) believe him?

    a. _____

    b. _____

▶ **Our friends and family will not always do what we do. Exemplify this by completing each sentence with a future tense verb form.**

5.5 a. Yo voy de vacaciones, pero mi mejor amigo no _____ de vacaciones.

   b. No vamos a visitarte, pero Guillermo te _____ .

   c. Tú no vas a pensar en eso, pero mis padres _____ en eso.

   d. Alejandro va a escribir el cheque, pero yo no lo _____ .

   e. Mis tías van a ir de compras, pero mis tíos no _____ de compras.

   f. Beto va a tener un postre, pero nosotras no _____ ningún postre.

   g. Uds. no van a saber todas las respuestas, pero ella siempre las _____ .

   h. Tú puedes cantar, pero yo no _____ cantar.

   i. Tu padre te va a dar un coche, pero mi padre nunca me _____ ninguno.

   j. Va a hacer frío hoy, y mañana _____ frío también.

▶ **Give the conditional form of each infinitive according to the subject given. Write out the entire verb form each time.**

5.6 1. nosotros

   a. arrancar _____

   b. masticar _____

   c. influir _____

2. tú

   a. crear _____

   b. subir _____

   c. vestirse _____

3. yo

   a. conducir _____

   b. dormirse _____

   c. beber _____

4. ellos

   a. encerrar _____

   b. mover _____

   c. partir _____

5. Ud.
   a. mostrar _____
   b. desear _____
   c. trabajar _____

6. yo
   a. encender _____
   b. aterrizar _____
   c. hervir _____

7. él
   a. ser _____
   b. dar _____
   c. volar _____

8. Uds.
   a. firmar _____
   b. ofrecer _____
   c. romper _____

▶ **Give the conditional form for each subject according to the infinitive given.**

5.7

1. hacer
   a. Consuelo _____
   b. las profesoras _____
   c. yo _____

2. ponerse
   a. Uds. y yo _____
   b. la Srta. Balón _____
   c. la familia Rodríguez _____

3. salir
   a. la clase _____
   b. los equipos _____
   c. yo _____

4. venir
   a. mis primos _____
   b. tu perro _____
   c. Uds. _____

5. tener
   a. el Sr. Macario _____
   b. tú _____
   c. tú y yo _____

6. decir
   a. yo _____
   b. los hermanos de Julieta _____
   c. el artículo _____

7. poder
   a. la compañía _____
   b. Ángel, Ana y Elisa _____
   c. yo _____

8. querer
   a. mi profesor _____
   b. las estudiantes _____
   c. Federico _____

9. valer
   a. el collar _____
   b. los aretes _____
   c. una casa nueva _____

10. saber
    a. yo _____
    b. mis abuelos y yo _____
    c. Uds. _____

Complete each translation with a conditional verb form.

5.8
a. She would need five dollars. _____ cinco dólares.

b. I wouldn't want any help. No _____ ninguna ayuda.

c. She would prefer to be alone. _____ estar sola.

d. Would you (friendly) see who is here? ¿_____ quién está aquí?

e. Would you like a drink? ¿Te _____ una bebida?

f. I have to go home now, or I would read the story to you. Tengo que ir a casa ahora, o te _____ el cuento.

g. They would set the table, but the dishes are broken. _____ la mesa, pero los platos están rotos.

h. Who could it be? ¿Quién _____ ser?

i. Could they speak a little louder? ¿_____ hablar un poco más alto?

j. She would never know the secret. No _____ nunca el secreto.

Give the future and conditional forms of the infinitives given.

5.9

	Future	Conditional
a. entretienen		
b. empiezo		
c. juega		
d. haces		
e. posee		
f. navegamos		
g. oigo		
h. impone		
i. están		
j. veo		

Answer the questions in complete Spanish sentences. Pay close attention to which tense you should use (the future or the conditional) in each of your responses.

5.10 a. ¿Cuándo tendrás veinte años?

_____

b. ¿Cuál de tus amigos será famoso? ¿Por qué?

_____

c. ¿Dónde te gustaría vivir como adulto(a)?

_____

d. ¿Qué regalo darás a tu mamá para la Navidad?

_____

e. ¿A qué hora te acostarás esta noche?

_____

f. ¿Qué harías con un millón de dólares?

_____

g. ¿Te casarás algún día?

_____

h. ¿Cómo podrías ayudar a un amigo en peligro?

_____

i. ¿Qué nota sacarás en el próximo examen? ¿Por qué?

_____

j. Para ti, ¿cómo sería un día perfecto?

_____

Complete the translations by filling in the missing vocabulary terms (from Unit Seven).

5.11 a. The airport is very far from here. _____ está _____ de aquí.

b. The flight attendant announces that passengers must fasten their seatbelts. _____ anuncia que los pasajeros deben _____ los cinturones de seguridad.

c. I have to stand in line. I hate to wait. Tengo que _____ . Yo odio _____ .

d. Please present your tickets. Favor de presentar _____ .

e. I bought a newspaper at the newsstand. Compré un periódico en el _____ .

f. The parking lot is full. Where can I park my car? _____ está lleno. ¿Dónde puedo _____ mi coche?

g. He's looking for his seat at the back of the plane. Busca su _____ al fondo del avión.

h. The pilot prepares himself for takeoff. _____ _____ para _____ .

i. We say good-bye before boarding the plane. _____ antes de _____ el avión.

j. I'm leaving from the airport. Salgo del _____ .

 Identify the following images in Spanish.

5.12

a. _____

b. _____

c. _____

d. _____

e. _____

f. _____

g. _____

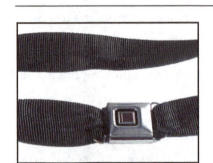
h. _____

i. _____

j. _____

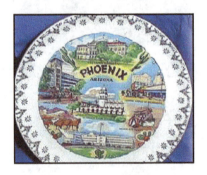
k. _____

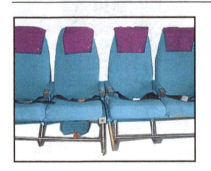
l. _____

m. _____

n. _____

o. _____

Circle the letter of the best answer to each question.

5.13

1. ¿Qué necesitas para saber a qué hora sale el avión?
   a. la sala de equipaje
   b. el horario
   c. el baño

2. ¿Quién pilotea el avión?
   a. la azafata
   b. la aduana
   c. el piloto

3. ¿Cómo te preparas para el despegue?
   a. visito la tienda de recuerdos
   b. busco la sala de equipaje
   c. me abrocho el cinturón de seguridad

4. ¿Adónde se puede ir por avión?
   a. al fondo
   b. a la cafetería
   c. al extranjero

5. ¿Qué haces con las maletas?
   a. facturo el equipaje
   b. desembarco del avión
   c. como en la cafetería

6. ¿A quién se puede pedir ayuda durante el vuelo?
   a. al piloto
   b. a la azafata
   c. a la aduana

7. ¿Qué hacen los pasajeros después del aterrizaje?
   a. estacionan
   b. bajan del avión
   c. obtienen los boletos

8. ¿Qué puedes hacer si el avión llega con retraso?
   a. miro la televisión
   b. llevo las maletas
   c. busco las maletas

9. ¿Dónde se muestra el pasaporte?
   a. en migración
   b. en la sala de equipaje
   c. en la tienda de recuerdos

10. ¿Qué hace Ud. cuando hay muchas personas en el mostrador de facturación?
    a. desembarco
    b. me preparo
    c. hago cola

Translate the following sentences into Spanish. Use the vocabulary from Unit Seven. Be careful to use the correct verb tenses.

5.14   a.   I will check my luggage. _____

       b.   We travel very far from here. _____

       c.   Present your (friendly) boarding pass to the flight attendant. _____

       d.   At the end of the flight, we get off the plane. _____

       e.   You (friendly) didn't see the pilot. _____

       f.   He visited the cafeteria because the flight arrived late. _____

       g.   She goes abroad by plane. _____

       h.   You (Ud.) will have to wait at the check-in counter. _____

       i.   My luggage is not in the baggage room. _____

       j.   He said good-bye to his girlfriend (*novia*) in the parking lot. _____

VI. GEOGRAPHY OF CENTRAL AMERICA AND THE CARIBBEAN

Use the information contained in these maps to help you complete the activities.

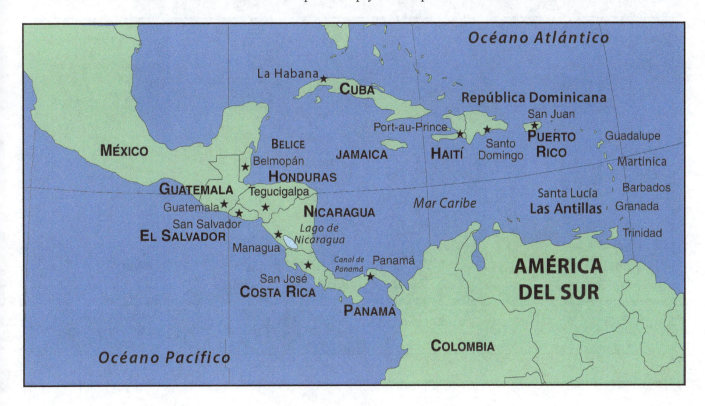

 Optional Activity: Create a map.

6.1 Create a room-sized map together. Try one of these two methods: Split the countries of Central America and the Caribbean up evenly among your students. Everyone will create, on posterboard, paper, even wood, etc. his particular countries. Be sure to include the capitals of each country. When all are complete, assemble them like a jigsaw puzzle on the wall and complete the map with labels of oceans, etc.

Join large sheets of posterboard to make one wall-sized poster. Draw the map directly onto it. Take turns labeling all the countries, capitals, and geographical features. Once you have completed the map, start paying closer attention to the world news section of your newspaper. Clip out relevant articles you find, even advertisements, and affix them to the pertinent countries on the wall map.

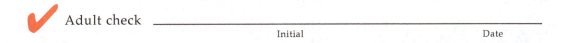

The map below illustrates the national languages of the countries of Central America and the Caribbean. There are many other dialects and native languages spoken in this region. For the sake of simplicity, only the national or dominant languages will be reviewed. There are three different languages that are widely used in this part of the world.

 Write a paper.

6.2 The diversity of language in this area reflects the history of Central America and the Caribbean. Choose one country and briefly investigate its history. Answer these questions.

   a. Who were the first Europeans to discover this country?

   b. For how long was this country under European control? Is it still today?

   c. If that European country relinquished control, which country took over? When and for how long?

   d. What language(s) was spoken prior to the arrival of the Europeans? Is that language(s) still alive today?

   Write a short one-page paper summarizing your findings. You may write the essay in English.

 Adult check _____
　　　　　　　　　　　　Initial　　　　　　　　　Date

POINTS OF INTEREST

Cuba. Cuba is the largest island country in this region. The United States occupies a naval base, Guantánamo, in this communist country. Cuba exports more sugar cane than any other Caribbean country. Other exports include: rice, coffee, cigars, citrus fruits, ebony, and mahogany. Cuba's economy was subsidized by the Soviet Union from the 1960s to the late 1980s when the Berlin Wall fell and communism collapsed in Europe. The government still owns most of the farmland and controls all foreign trade. Recently, doors have been opened to the practice of Christianity, and the churches in Cuba are growing.

**República Dominicana.** Located on the eastern two-thirds of the island of Hispaniola, the Dominican Republic is home to the New World's oldest university, the University of Santo Domingo. This island began as a Spanish colony, but it was taken over by the French. In 1697, Spain ceded the western portion (Haiti) to France. Today, the Dominican Republic is a hybrid of French and Spanish influences, with Spanish being the primary language spoken. The Dominican Republic exports sugar cane and cacao beans (for the manufacture of chocolate). Other exports include pineapple, citrus fruit, tobacco, silver, bauxite, and nickel.

**Panamá.** In 1903, the Panama Canal Treaty granted the United States the right to build the canal. In 1914, the canal was completed. The Panama Canal provides fast and safe passage from the Atlantic to the Pacific, as opposed to traveling all the way around the southern tip of South America. Because of numerous disputes between Panama and the United States regarding sovereignty issues, the United States enacted another treaty in 1977 which relinquished control to the Panamanians in 2000. The Isthmus of Panama connects North and South America. The Canal technically separates the two continents. Bananas and rice are primary exports from Panama. Many Panamanians are bilingual, speaking both Spanish and English.

**Costa Rica.** When Spanish explorers first settled the region, they were hoping to find gold and other valuable minerals—hence the name, *Costa Rica* or "rich coast." The official language there is Spanish. Roughly 90 percent of the population is composed of practicing Roman Catholics. Their legal system is based on Spanish law. Costa Rica gained independence from Spain in 1821 and now practices a democratic republican system of government. Costa Rica is also well-known for its rain forests. For that reason, it is becoming an increasingly popular tourist destination. It is primarily an agrarian country that exports coffee, bananas, textiles, sugar, rice, corn, and beans.

**Honduras.** Honduras is the second largest nation in Central America, as well as the poorest. This country shares many of the same cultural influences of the Spanish explorers with its neighbors. The primary language is Spanish, and the legal system is based on Spanish law. The name of Honduras's capital, Tegucigalpa, is a native word meaning "silver hill." Honduras exports this mineral, as well as bananas, coffee, beef, timber, and shrimp.

**El Salvador.** El Salvador, which means *the Savior*, is known as the Land of Volcanoes. The capital, San Salvador, is famous for the Santa Ana volcano. Like much of Central America, this country is mountainous, the terrain having been created by volcanic activity. El Salvador is Central America's smallest country and the only one without a coastline on the Caribbean Sea. El Salvador has very good natural resources such as hydroelectric power, geothermal power, petroleum, and arable land. Coffee is this country's main export. Other exports include sugar, shrimp, beef and dairy products, cotton, and offshore assembly products.

**Guatemala.** Guatemala was ruled by Spain until 1821. After that, there were many different ruling factions vying for control of the country. In 1996, 36 years of civil war were ended, opening the country up to greater foreign investment and opportunities. Sixty percent of the population speaks Spanish, with forty percent speaking over twenty different Amerindian languages. Many Mayan ruins

are found in Guatemala, particularly the ancient deserted city of Tikal. Natural resources in Guatemala include petroleum, nickel, rare woods, and chicle (for chewing gum). Over half of the population is employed in agriculture, with the main exports being sugar, coffee, and bananas. Other exports include meat, petroleum, and apparel.

Puerto Rico. Puerto Rico is a self-governing commonwealth of the United States, located just east of Hispaniola. It is not an independent country; however, they have their own constitution which has to be approved by the United States. People of Puerto Rico are considered American citizens. The head of state is the President of the United States, and Puerto Ricans celebrate the Fourth of July with the rest of America. There are cultural differences, however. Spanish is the major language, due to the country's heritage as a Spanish colony, but 65 percent of the population speak English as a second language. The Spanish influence is evident in the architecture. Their legal system is based on Spanish law. Puerto Rico exports a variety of products, including coffee, sugar cane, pharmaceuticals, electronics, apparel, canned tuna, and medical equipment.

Nicaragua. Nicaragua is the largest country of Central America. It features Lake Nicaragua, the largest inland body of water in Central America. Nicaragua is also one of the poorest of the Central American countries. Early in this country's history, English, Dutch, and French pirates used this country as a hideout, raiding Spanish plantations and attacking Spanish shipping in the Caribbean. Plantations produce coffee and sugar cane for export. Other exports include shrimp and lobster, cotton, beef, tobacco, bananas, and gold.

▶ **Fill in the blanks (in English) regarding all the information you have just studied.**

6.3 a. _____ is the largest island country of this region.

b. _____ is the largest country of Central America.

c. The Republic of Haiti shares an island with _____ .

d. _____ is the continent to the north of Caribbean region, while _____ is to the south.

e. The Caribbean islands to the east of Cuba and the Dominican Republic are called the _____ .

f. _____ is a group of countries forming an isthmus, or land bridge, between the greater portion of North America and South America.

g. _____ and _____ join Central America to North America.

h. _____ joins Central America to South America.

i. The people of _____ are considered American citizens.

j. The _____ Ocean is on the western side of Central America.

Match the countries with their capitals.

6.4
1. _____ Puerto Rico
2. _____ República Dominicana
3. _____ Guatemala
4. _____ Costa Rica
5. _____ Panamá
6. _____ Honduras
7. _____ Cuba
8. _____ Nicaragua
9. _____ El Salvador

a. Guatemala
b. La Habana
c. Panamá
d. Managua
e. San Juan
f. San José
g. San Salvador
h. Tegucigalpa
i. Santo Domingo

 Map activities.

6.5 Label the color-coded map on page 82 with the the names of the appropriate countries.

 Adult check _____
　　　　　　　　　　　　　　　Initial　　　　　　　　　　　Date

6.6 Label the above map. Include the names of the countries and their capitals, as well as bodies of water. Do as much as you can from memory before referring to your notes.

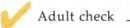 Adult check _____
　　　　　　　　　　　　　　　Initial　　　　　　　　　　　Date

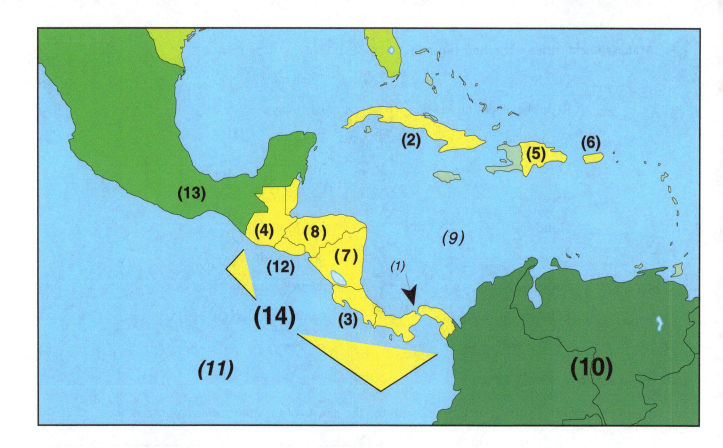

 Write the number of each country or geographical feature described below.

6.7
a. Continent that connects with Panama. _____

b. Exports the most sugar cane of this region. _____

c. Country whose capital means "silver hill." _____

d. Country directly north of Guatemala. _____

e. Home of the Western Hemisphere's oldest university. _____

f. Body of water to the west of the Panama Canal. _____

g. Country popular with tourists for its lush rain forests. _____

h. Body of water that is home to Cuba, Hispaniola, and Puerto Rico. _____

i. Island territory of the United States. _____

j. Largest country of Central America. _____

k. Man-made waterway that connects the Pacific and Atlantic Oceans. _____

l. Home of the Mayan ruins of Tikal. _____

m. Tiny Central American country known for a large volcano. _____

n. Group of countries that forms an isthmus between Mexico and Colombia. _____

Complete the crossword puzzle.

6.8

ACROSS

3. capital city of Guatemala
6. ancient Mayan ruins in Guatemala
8. capital city of Belice
9. capital city of Honduras
11. capital city of Panamá
12. capital city of the República Dominicana
14. capital city of El Salvador
15. capital city of Haiti

DOWN

1. capital city of Cuba
2. volcano of El Salvador
4. translation of "Tegucigalpa"
5. popular export of Central America
7. primary language spoken in Haiti
10. capital city of Costa Rica
13. capital city of Nicaragua

Optional Activity: For further study.

At this point, you may wish to further investigate one specific country. This is an optional exercise designed to enhance your insight into this part of the world. One to two pages should be sufficient. Some suggestions are:

1. The early explorations of the Europeans and their effect on the native peoples.

2. The history of the Mayan people and their presence today.

3. Political upheaval and unrest (especially appropriate for Guatemala, Nicaragua, and El Salvador).

4. Eco-tourism, vacationing, sightseeing, and the rain forest (especially good for Puerto Rico and Costa Rica).

5. The history and development of the Panama Canal Zone.

6. History of plantations, slavery, and the sugar industry.

VOCABULARY LIST
[CD–E, Track 13]

NOUNS
el aceite – the oil
el acelerador – the accelerator (gas pedal)
el asiento de delante – the front seat
el asiento trasero – the back seat
el auto – the car
el automóvil – the car
el baúl – the trunk
la bocina – the horn
el carro – the car
la cerradura – the lock
el cinturón de seguridad – the seat belt
el claxon – the horn
el coche – the car
el conductor – the driver
la esquina – the corner
el faro – the headlight
los frenos – the brakes
la gasolina – the gasoline
la gasolinera – the gas station
el intermitente – the turn signal (both inside and outside the car)
la ley – the law
el limpiaparabrisas – the windshield wiper
la llanta – the tire
la luz – the (dome) light
la mensualidad – the monthly payment
el motor – the engine
la multa – the ticket, fine
la oscuridad – the darkness
el parabrisas – the windshield
el parachoques – the bumper
el préstamo – the loan
la puerta – the door
la radio – the radio
la rueda – the wheel
el tanque – the (gas) tank
la velocidad – the speed
la ventanilla – the (car) window
el volante – the steering wheel

VERBS
abrir – to open
abrocharse el cinturón de seguridad – to fasten one's seat belt
acelerar – to accelerate
adquirir (i-ie) – to acquire
alquilar – to rent
arrancar – to start (car)
arreglar – to fix
arrendar (e-ie) – to rent
aumentar la velocidad – to increase speed, speed up
avisar – to warn
cambiar el aceite – to change the oil
cerrar (e-ie) – to close
chocarse con – to crash into
conducir – to drive
dar un paseo – to go for a ride
devolver (o-ue) – to return (something)
dirigir – to steer, direct
doblar (la esquina) – to turn (the corner)
echar gasolina en el coche – to put gas in the car
encender (e-ie) – to light; turn on (light, turn signal)
entretener – to entertain
evitar – to avoid
fallar – to fail (referring to brakes)
funcionar (bien/mal) – to function/work (well/badly) (refers to machines)
guiar – to steer
iluminar – to illuminate, light (up)
impedir (e-i) las heridas – to prevent injuries
lavar – to wash
limpiar – to clean
llenar el tanque – to fill the tank
llevar – to carry
manejar – to drive
mantener – to maintain
mostrar (o-ue) – to show
obedecer las leyes – to obey the laws
obtener – to get, obtain
pagar a plazos – to make (monthly) payments
parar – to stop (+ noun)
pararse – to stop oneself
pedir (e-i) prestado – to borrow
prestar – to loan
prestar atención – to pay attention
proteger – to protect
quitar – to take away, remove
reducir la velocidad – to reduce speed, slow down
reparar – to repair
romper – to break
señalar – to signal
tener cuidado – to be careful
tocar la bocina/el claxon – to honk the horn
virar – to turn, swerve

ADJECTIVES AND ADVERBS
demasiado – too, too much
peligroso – dangerous
por dentro – inside, in the interior
ya – already

PREPOSITIONS
a la derecha de – to the right of
a la izquierda de – to the left of
al fondo de –at the back of
alrededor de – around
cerca de – near
debajo de – under
dentro de – inside of

en – in, on
en la parte delantera de – in the front part
en medio de – in the middle of
encima de – on top of
entre – between, among
junto a – next to
lejos de – far from
sobre – on